Love Letters

From the Heart

Compiled By
Tracy Ruckman

ISBN-13: 978-0-9991503-9-9
E-book ISBN: 978-0-9991503-2-0

Originally Published by Pix-N-Pens ©2012

Published by TMP Books, 1420 Martha Berry Blvd, Unit 1241, Rome, GA 30165
www.TMPbooks.com

To order additional copies of this resource online, visit www.TMPbooks.com.

Cover Designed by Suzanne Williams.

Printed in the United States of America.

Dear Reader,

My grandmother gave me a love of letters. Quickly penned or days spent journaling – her letters always touched something deep inside me, and made me feel loved in a special way.

Within these pages, you'll discover hearts poured out over stories that may resemble your own.

We pray these letters touch your life in a special way, and that the changed lives of the letter writers reveal a depth of God's love that you may not have experienced before. It is our hope that you experience Him now in a new and afresh, and that your life will be forever changed.

You are deeply, richly, unconditionally loved.

I promise.

There is no one righteous, not even one;
there is no one who understands,
no one who seeks God.
All have turned away,
they have together become worthless;
there is no one who does good,
not even one.

Romans 3:10-12

For all have sinned and
fall short of the glory of God ...

Romans 3:23

For the wages of sin is death,
but the gift of God is
eternal life
in Christ Jesus our Lord.

Romans 6:23

My children,

After more than thirty-five years, the memory is still vivid. You don't remember much; you were very young at the time, but I want you to understand what happened.

Your father, like my own mother and father, was an alcoholic. And, like them, he was a functional alcoholic. He could work all week, but on weekends, he became drunk. Too many weekends passed like this, and one day, I couldn't take any more. I decided to leave.

He came home from work that Friday evening with bloodshot eyes, and a slur in his speech. I gathered my courage and told him I was leaving. I could see the anger in his eyes, simmering just beneath the surface.

"Don't bother," he said, "I'll leave." With that statement, he went to the bedroom and began throwing underwear into a suitcase. The air popped with electricity as I struggled to control my ragged breathing. I found it hard to believe all the one-nighters would stop; and all the abuse would finally end. The afternoon he kicked your brother in the back brought me to tears. Not to mention all the degrading things he said to me, or the holes he punched in the walls, or the dog he tried to kick.

Your father threw some more things in the suitcase, and then turned to face me. Etched across his face was a rage I'd never seen. I knew better than to say anything. I simply watched as he closed the bedroom doors and locked the windows. My throat clutched. He walked into the closet. In one hand, he brought out a shiny, black gun. In the other, he held a box of bullets.

He loaded the bullets into the gun's cylinder. Each round clicked into the chamber, and I measured my life in each one.

As a young adult, I had walked away from the God I knew as a child. I felt I knew better than He did how to run my life. Like my parents and husband, I found solace in drinking. The only time I felt really in control, and safe, was when I had a drink. Later, I realized that drinking was my way of escaping all the pain and anguish in my life. Nothing in my childhood, or in my marriage, was normal; it was all dysfunctional.

Your father aimed the gun at my stomach. I knew he fully intended to kill me—and himself. That was when I silently cried out to God. Lord, I don't want to die. Please let me see my children grow up. It was in that instant that I felt God encourage me to tell my husband I loved him. I did love him; I just didn't think I could live with him any longer.

"I love you," I said.

"I don't believe you," he shot back, his eyes blazing.

"I do. I'm not leaving." I held my breath as he slowly lowered the gun. I didn't know just how close I had come to dying until later. While sitting beside him late that evening, he told me exactly what he had planned to do. After learning of his twisted, detailed plans, I knew I could never stay.

The following months, after I left, were harrowing for me; for us. I don't know if you knew, but a recession was in full force and jobs were scarce. I finally found a part-time job, but didn't bring in enough to feed and house all of us. Your dad only paid one child support payment, and that was all. So, we ended up on welfare, until I could find full-time work.

I was thankful for simply being alive. I searched for peace, for relief from the fear I experienced, even after he found us again, and slapped me around, busting my lip and bruising my face. The fear became so great that I slept downstairs on a sofa, fully clothed, with a loaded gun under my pillow. Fear hounded me every day for a year.

He followed me once to work, and grabbed my arm, threatening to take me somewhere with him. I put up such a protest that he turned me loose. These unexpected occurrences happened so often that I felt the specter of fear around every corner. I cowered whenever I saw a man who favored him. Unless you've been through it, it's hard to understand that kind of pervasive fear—fear, in the form of someone you once loved, stalking you. Tears well up now, even thinking about it.

But one day several years after I married your stepfather, I decided to take both of you, and your younger sister and brother to church. (I had to persuade "Dad" to go; and months later, he went too.)

As I read the Bible, and began praying, I found peace—the peace that passes all understanding. I learned to call God my Father, even my "Daddy," which brought such joy I cannot begin to tell you.

You need to understand I never had a real daddy, who loved me like God. I didn't have anyone to hold me close during my trials; to even emotionally let me know I was loved. I never heard the words "I love you" from either of my parents. Alcoholics are selfish people.

When I learned the suffering that Jesus experienced on the cross—the nails, the thorns, the pierced side—for me and my sins; I could barely believe it. He took my sins, from my past, my present, and get this, even my future, upon him that dark day on the cross. Once I asked forgiveness of my sins, He freed me from them. I accepted His free gift of salvation, and now I am free! I am free from that anguish and pain of domestic violence! I am free from ever depending on alcohol again. I am free from that fear that ran my life! Jesus paid the price for me on the cross. I am His child. My name is written in the palm of His hand. I feel such joy and love, knowing I belong to Him.

Peter says in 1 Peter 1:3, which I have paraphrased, that in his great mercy, Jesus has given us new birth (I was born again!) into a living hope through the resurrection of Jesus Christ from the dead, and into an inheritance that can never perish, spoil or fade—kept in heaven for you (and for me!). Through faith in Jesus, I am born again, into Him, and into an inheritance that no one can ever take from me, and God is keeping it in heaven for me. What joy I feel!

Know you are always on my heart and mind. I love you.

Mom

Just Dear Survivor,

How could a loving God allow such a horrible thing to happen? Maybe He just doesn't care, so He's not loving. Or, if He cares, then maybe He doesn't have the power to help and He's not really God.

Have you ever felt that way? I've been there— trust me!

I came to Christ as an adult, searching for love and acceptance. But I sort of walled God off from the past pain, and from the present effects of it, too. Because that past awfulness does change the present. There's no getting around it, but I couldn't figure out how God made a difference. I just couldn't make it work, in my head.

Sometimes well-intentioned people would say, "God was with you when it happened!" Give me a break! What good is it to that frightened child, like I was, to know God was standing around watching her be hurt?

I knew, and I know, that God is not the author of evil (James 1:13, 1 Corinthians 14:33). I also know He cares when I'm hurt (1 Peter 5:7, Psalm 147:3).

But ... I couldn't figure out how that changed what happened to me. Do you know what I mean?

Then I went to a praise service after the Columbine massacre in 1999. The leader, Dennis Jernigan, talked about the times when we wonder, where was God? How could He allow that to happen? Dennis asked us to remember a time when those questions were strong, and to try to see Jesus in the situation. I thought it was silly, but I obediently closed my eyes and called up what little I can recall of the first time I was hurt so badly.

To my surprise, I was overwhelmed with feelings of sorrow and compassion for my mother! At some childish level, I'd always blamed her for leaving me vulnerable to the assault. That evening, God gave me understanding that she hadn't intentionally left me helpless, that she was doing the best she could. Did it change the incident itself? Of course not! But a great deal of the sting and resentment was gone.

Recently a teen-aged friend disclosed that her father had been sexually abusing her. In all the confusion of the next few weeks—short-term, out-of-home placement for the girl, interviews by police and social workers, questions and anger and fear from her siblings and mother, her father's arrest—she and I made time to talk quietly.

"Do you remember your abuse?" was her first question. I answered, "I remember some of it. And a lot of what I remember is … well, from the ceiling, watching as if it happened to someone else." She was silent a moment, then said, "That's how I remember what he did." She had doubted her own perceptions, and my past trauma had validated her feelings.

The prophet Joel wrote God's warning to Israel, followed by His promise to redeem their suffering and turn evil to good: What the locust swarm has left, the great locusts have eaten; what the great locusts have left, the young locusts have eaten; what the young locusts have left, other locusts have eaten. … I will repay you for the years the locusts have eaten— the great locust and the young locust, the other locusts and the locust swarm—my great army that I sent among you. You will have plenty to eat, until you are full, and you will praise the name of the LORD your God, who has worked wonders for you (Joel 1:4; 2:25-26).

God didn't cause your abuse. But He will take it and turn it to good, if you let Him. I know, because He's done it for me. Empathy for my mother ... a connection with a fellow sufferer ... God does indeed bring good from evil.

In God's love,

Someone Who's Been There

Dear Shy Person,

I feel for you. It's not easy being born shy. Scared to talk to people, scared to even meet their eyes. As a young child, I hid behind my mom's skirt when she chatted with people. As I grew older, that obviously wouldn't do. I needed to converse with people on my own. So I began to make a friend here and there who were near my age. It was pretty easy to talk with them once I got to know them. Adults ... well, if I had to, I could answer their questions. But I certainly wouldn't initiate conversation.

By the time I was in middle school, I was okay talking with adults I knew. For instance, if I needed to ask one of the teachers at our home school co-op a question, I could. But expect me to go to a customer service desk and ask something or order ice cream by myself ... no way! I think the underlying fear has always been: What if I say the wrong thing? What if I make a fool of myself?

It's simple for someone to say, "Don't care about what men think of you. Focus on God. Then you won't be afraid."

It's not so simple to put into practice. Anyone who is naturally outgoing doesn't understand the paralyzing fear. Thinking I can't do this.

Then, your body betrays you! For some, it's tears. For others, it's blushing. For me? My arms and legs start shaking uncontrollably. It's not fun.

Yes, shy people – as well as those who aren't shy – should focus on God. Yes, we shouldn't care what people think about us. But that does not mean we will automatically lose our shyness or fear. It may mean, however, that we can speak up and do what we should even though we are afraid. This should never be attempted in our own strength. We need to depend on God.

My mom let me know about a speech/apologetics club that was starting in our town, my senior year of homeschool high school. I wanted to be better at public speaking (i.e. be able to do it without shaking or in any other way having a nervous breakdown). And although apologetics is wonderful, I still thought this just wasn't my thing. Mom said that the first night the family would show the different kinds of speeches they would be teaching and give anyone interested the opportunity to get to know them. I didn't have to make a decision yet. So I went. I was impressed at the level of skill the young adults displayed. I thought it looked fun ... in a way. In the end, I joined.

I learned the difference between an illustrative oratory and a persuasive oratory, the difference between a duo presentation and a presentation using apologetics cards. On speech presentation night, I gave two speeches. One was an apologetics speech, which covered misconceptions surrounding Christ's propitiation. The other was a ten-minute illustrative oratory about why Christians must be involved in reaching the unreached with the Gospel. Two pretty radical – and perhaps to some, even uncomfortable – topics. Yet, in a way, that helped me because I believe in both strongly. When I am passionate about something, I'm more willing to take risks. In this case, I was willing to risk humiliation, but thankfully, it went well.

God has brought me far and I am so thankful for His grace. It feels ridiculous to admit that when I called customer service for the first time, my voice quivered a bit. It was pathetic. The guy who took my call was located in India, and although he answers hundreds of phone calls a day, my nerves still refused to completely cooperate. But I persevered because they had messed up on a product and I knew I'd never have to meet this person face-to-face.

Fast forward to preparations for my first mission trip this last summer. I had to make dozens of phone calls. I wanted to go badly enough that I was willing to step out of my comfort zone doing simple things most people take for granted. Things like scheduling an appointment by phone to get my passport. This was the first time I'd ever had to make an appointment. Other phone calls included calling a notary public, a nurse, and several travel agents. After doing it a few times, I realized it wasn't so bad. My graduation from homeschool high school was held at a local church a few weeks before my mission trip. Since I was the only graduate, I would be giving a speech. I expected my old nerves to come back and haunt me as I got up on stage to deliver my speech. I prayed that I would do well and not be nervous, though. Guess what? God enabled me to be peaceful and even relax enough to have fun with it!

During my mission trip, I served for seven-and-a-half weeks onboard the Logos Hope while she was docked in Malaysia. I was given the opportunity to share my salvation testimony with a group of children in an aboriginal jungle village there.

Me! The girl who was born shy but has a reason to speak so huge and so important that even though she's not fearless, she's willing to do her best and leave the rest up to God. To God alone be the glory.

My shyness has often seemed a hindrance. It's been an obstacle. But I realize now that it can also be a testimony to the power and grace of God.

May His strength always be made perfect in our weakness!

Soli Deo Gloria,
No Longer Speechless

Dear Summer Sidekick,

Thank you so much for the sweet card that you sent me when my Dad died a few months ago. For several years, I wanted to send you a note but life is so busy! Now, after the pain of my Dad's parting has subsided, your thoughtfulness in sending the card prompts me to respond. The memories of our childhood, playing together on the farm, continue to warm my heart even though we haven't been in close contact as grownups.

Remember when the first tomatoes of the season ripened? Everybody knew it – it was a very special day! The evening before, while we were getting cleaned up, Dad went out to the garden and inspected the ripening fruit. An experienced gardener, he knew the importance of one more night and day on the vine.

Coming back into the house, he made the solemn proclamation, "Tomorrow night, we'll have tomatoes." My heart smiles at the memory of you and me clapping our hands and hugging each other in anticipation. Our moms agreed that you could be a participant in this planned treat; even allowing you to sleepover. Such a sweet memory of our friendship!

The next night, after the tomatoes had one last day to ripen, we didn't eat supper at the usual time. We waited until sunset. As the setting sun turned the sky to scarlet and the clouds began to glow purple, mom fried the thick-cut bacon while Dad sharpened his big tomato cutting knife.

As he worked, he explained to us the importance of a very sharp knife. If the blade wasn't razor sharp, the tomatoes would smash instead of slice. Every country girl knows that a smashed tomato has a totally different flavor than a sliced tomato! With every swish on the sharpening stone, our mouths watered a little more.

Finally, the knife sharper than a surgeon's scalpel, Daddy leaned over with knife poised and said, "Everybody ready?" We hovered at the edge of the counter top where the red-enough-to-bust-open tomato lay waiting. Dad made the first cut and the fragrance of that dead ripe tomato flew up into our faces like a warm fog! We shut our eyes, rocked back on our heels, and moaned, 'Mmmm.'

My youngest brother was too little to help much,

but he carefully took the bread out of the bag and handed us the slices. You and I made the toasted white bread and smeared on the mayonnaise. We carefully made sure the thick white mayonnaise went corner-to-corner, edge-to-edge. My mom said you could tell if a person was generous or stingy by the way they put mayonnaise on a slice of bread!

Sandwiches made, we all went outside, each of us carrying a plate of bacon and tomato sandwiches and a glass of sweet tea. The glasses of sweet tea were so cold that the glasses were sweating on the outside! Mom spread a quilt on the ground and we all sat on it to eat the sandwiches. This being the first tomatoes of the season, we ate as many as we wanted; mom made lots of them!

After eating as many sandwiches as we could hold, we ran around catching fire flies as they blinked in the fading evening light. Later, we lay on the blanket looking at the stars twinkling in the sky. Dad pointed out all the constellations and told jokes to make us laugh. His favorite jokes were always the ones about the chicken crossing the road. We fell asleep laughing and woke up the next morning, in bed, never remembering having gotten there.

A lifetime later, I sat with my Dad as he lay dying. The last trip to the doctor had delivered the dreaded news. In spite of all that modern technology and medicine could do, the race was over. The cancer had won. Now, I waited for the suffering to be done and heaven to be the last and final victor.

Daddy lay so thin, so pale. His wasted body barely made a rise beneath the blanket; we talked of youth, childhood, laughter, and the first tomato sandwiches. Even in the pain of death, he told me jokes, saying, "I'll tell the jokes, but you do the laughing, honey, because I'm too weak, ok?"

We talked about what joke he was going to tell Jesus first. Dad decided on "Why did the chicken cross the road?" because Jesus would know the real answer.

As another last day drew to a close, I did my best to make Daddy comfortable. I asked him if I could fix him anything to eat before he settled down to sleep. His appetite gone, his 'innards' as he called them, unable to digest any food at all, he said, "Not now, but, tomorrow, I hope the tomatoes will be ripe and you can bring me a tomato sandwich."

A few days later, Daddy went home to Jesus. My heart knows that he is eating his longed for first-of-the-season tomato sandwich – with his precious Savior.

With tears on my face, I ask you, if you were to die today, my friend, would you be sitting with Jesus?

If you can't say you would be, pray this prayer with me, "Heavenly Father, I realize that I'm a sinner and that Jesus died on the cross to save me. I ask for forgiveness and accept the blood of Christ as covering for my sins. Thank you and please help me, through your Holy Spirit, to live for you each day. I love you, Lord."

Please continue to stay in close contact and, if you prayed that prayer, I'll see you in heaven someday. We'll be eating the best ever tomato sandwich, with my sweet Daddy.

Love the Lord like a child.

Your Childhood Friend

Dear High School Confidante,

I hope you are feeling better than when we spoke. It was a real surprise, running into you after all these years. I enjoyed our short visit, though it stirred many memories I'd rather not recall.

As you briefly mentioned some of your current problems, I tried to offer encouragement and comfort. Yet afterwards I was concerned that my life as you knew me in high school probably lent little credence to my words. That concern prompted this letter, and I hope you'll be gracious enough to receive its message.

First of all, I must explain that, in my pre-teen years, I had genuinely received Christ. At that time it was a sincere and joyful experience, though I had a limited concept of it. I understood the basics: that I was indeed a sinner, and that Jesus loved me and died to save me. I confessed my sins and received Him as Savior. Unfortunately, it was much later that I learned He was not only Savior, but also Lord, with a claim on my life and a purpose for it. Neither did I know anything about getting His daily strength to carry all that out.

I spent the next decade wavering between frustration at being unable to live up to the Christian life I'd imagined, and that stubborn nature in me that really wanted to do my own thing anyway. Gradually I leaned more and more to the latter, becoming the person you knew in our teenage years. Though mercifully God kept me from disaster, my rebellion and willful, independent spirit gave a poor example of a Christian life. My selfishness, disregard for others, and scorn for guidelines left impressions and influence that can never be changed. I even recall knowing that your home life was hard because of the effects of alcoholism, but I was insensitive, and probably even acted "superior" toward you.

You may know that I was married soon after high school and plunged into adult life. As it quickly became too much for me, I learned a whole new way. It is that I want to share with you.

I acquired a husband, a baby son, then a daughter, all before my twenty-first birthday. At about that time, my mother became ill with cancer. Because Mom had been the spiritual leader and strength of our family, this news rocked my world. When she died a few months later, I began to fall apart. Added to my grief, was heavy guilt because of my rebellion and general attitudes, as I'd strayed from lots of the principles Mom had taught me. Suddenly I knew I needed God. Imagine my alarm when I couldn't find Him. I cried out to Him, but it was like my voice was unheard, in a vacuum. I tried attending a local church, tried various antidepressants, but nothing helped the emptiness and guilt. My husband and children suffered greatly from the agony in which I found myself.

At this point, God sent into my life a gracious, godly lady who enlisted me in a Bible class and began to teach me, mentor me, and pray for me. She also prayed for my home and family, by then on the verge of a break-up.

The light began to dawn as I was finally desperate enough to be open to God's way and His Word. I was taught many wonderful truths. Among them was the fact that He had never left me but I'd left Him. I found that His forgiveness covered all my sins; He was only waiting for me to acknowledge them and ask.

I learned that God had created me with love and purpose, that He had a wonderful plan for my life. He had given His Word and His Holy Spirit to help me experience that. The things I couldn't do, the people I couldn't love, He was more than able to handle. Not only was it possible, but it was what He wanted for me. I found immense relief in discovering this and in turning everything over to Him.

It was here that the real change took place in my life. God's comfort and love daily flowed into my life and with them a fresh desire to live to please Him. To put it another way, He turned me upside down, dumped out the bad stuff little by little, and poured His good stuff in. First my heart, then my life and my home were transformed.

Many years later, that process is still taking place. As a very old song says, "Through many dangers, toils, and snares I have already come. T'was grace that brought me safe thus far and grace will lead me home."

That's why I can now tell you with absolute confidence that God is sufficient for your problems as

He is for mine. He is waiting for you to seek Him with all your heart. He's interested, first of all, in you, then in your needs and problems. Start with that sweet relationship with Him, which in itself satisfies your inner need. Then move on to that daily walk through all of life, good and bad, and keep knowing Him better. It's a great adventure.

Please forgive me if this sounds "preachy." That's definitely not my intention. It all simply comes from my heart.

Please call me at any time, if you'd like to talk about any of this. At seventeen, I thought I had all the answers. Now I know I have none, but I know the One Who does!

If you'd like, you can just update me on how things are going for you. It's a privilege and a joy to have a second chance to touch your life.

With love,

Your "New" Old Friend

Precious Friend,

I am writing this letter because I know you are in a difficult place. I want to share about a difficult time in my life and what changed me forever.

The easiest way to describe my journey is to tell you about the unrealistic expectations I had for my life from the age of ten. It all began with the movie Cinderella. From that point on I figured all my expectations would automatically materialize. I wanted to excel, I wanted to go to college, have a stellar career, make a lot of money, fall in love with Prince Charming someday and have a wedding most girls only dream about. Of course, I also wanted a beautiful home, the finer things of life, and I wanted children. Add to that plenty of money, lavish vacations, children who made me look good and a long and happy life. I believed that one day I would die and gloriously exit into heaven with all my make-up in place. Why plan for anything less?

My plans suddenly changed when I was 15. My dad was fired from his very public job. His picture was on the front page of our newspaper.

Unbeknownst to me, dad was fired because he had a drinking problem. We were so humiliated we moved out of town a few months later. But daddy kept on drinking. He lost more jobs than he kept. On the day of my high school graduation, he left us a suicide note. He claimed he couldn't stop drinking. He told us that when we found his body we'd get the insurance money and be financially secure. I was gripped with fear and my Mom fell apart. That night, in a very vulnerable state of mind, I fell into the arms of my high-school sweetheart, my prince charming, and my life was never the same.

A few weeks later dad came home. He'd been on a drunken binge in Mexico and lost what little money we had. Two months later I learned I was pregnant. I knew my parents would be disgraced. I was right!

Desperate and disappointed, we got married a few weeks later in a dimly lit chapel with no friends, flowers, or festivities. We moved into a one room apartment by the university, complete with hot and cold running rats. My husband started college and I started working until our baby arrived. I had to go back to work two months later to put food on the table while my husband went to school full time and four years later he finally got out. But two months after graduation, he left me a note on the kitchen table. He said he needed to get away and 'find himself.' He wasn't sure what he wanted to do. Within days, I learned I was pregnant again. I wanted to run away too. Instead, I moved home with my parents. A few weeks before I was due to deliver, my husband begged me to forgive him and take him back. I didn't want to, but I was in desperate straits. So we reconciled and tried to make things work, but we were miserable. I lived in constant fear he would leave again.

Soon a movement came on the scene promising fearful women they could be liberated from miserable marriages. I sat up and listened. I began thinking what I needed was a new prince, hopefully a charming one.

But before I could carry out my plan, a friend showed up one afternoon for a visit and a cup of coffee. She asked if she could share something with me that would explain why my circumstances seemed so hopeless. I leaned forward and said, "Yes!" She began to share the Gospel with me from a small tract.

Before she turned to the second page, tears began streaming down my face. When she reached the end of that little booklet I was weeping. Jesus was knocking at the door of my heart and I couldn't wait to ask Him to come in. He did!

When I waved good-bye to my friend, I realized something dramatic had happened to me. First, my eyes fell on two precious children. I felt a love for them I'd never had. Then my husband came home and I felt the ice start to melt around my hard heart. He asked what had happened to me and I told him.

Within three months, my prince gave his life to the King and Jesus began to resurrect our dead marriage from the graveyard. Within weeks, we began to fall in love with each other all over again. Jesus was transforming our lives.

This new life began many years ago. It took place during the last great revival in America, sometimes referred to as the Jesus Movement.

This year we are celebrating 50 years of marriage. I have learned there is nothing wrong with expectations, but when you compare them to knowing Jesus Christ, they only satisfy short term.

Affectionately,

New Expectations

But God demonstrates his own love for us in this:
While we were still sinners, Christ died for us.
Romans 5:8

That if you confess with your mouth, "Jesus is Lord,"
and believe in your heart that God raised him from
the dead, you will be saved. For it is with your heart
that you believe and are justified, and it is with your
mouth that you confess and are saved.
Romans 10:9-10

"Everyone who calls on the name of the Lord
will be saved."
Romans 10:13

Dear Student,

Congratulations on your acceptance to college. We are so proud of your accomplishments and your decision to seek higher education. I state that with heartfelt sincerity, yet I want to caution you too.

As a college instructor, I've seen a wide range of attitudes and behavior in students. Those who are likely to pass the courses I teach are not only students who possess an easy grasp of the subject, but also those students for whom the subject is challenging yet they persist in their attempts. Persistence isn't just about showing up for classes, doing the assigned work, and participating in activities; it is making the choice to commit to the coursework despite the difficulties.

Even if I could wish you easy understanding of all your courses, I would not do so, because there is value in the struggle to grasp a difficult concept. We appreciate what we work hard for. As noted in Luke 6:38, Give, and it will be given to you. A good measure, pressed down, shaken together and running over, will be poured into your lap. For with the measure you use, it will be measured to you.

Enjoy what comes effortlessly to you, but welcome the struggle to gain control of those ideas that are elusive.

Not everyone passes a course, but every single student could pass. Unfortunately, some students let a false sense of entitlement hamper their educational goals. They assume that their acceptance into college means they're capable. They become complacent about their easy enrollment, thinking they're in for an easy ride to their diploma. I worry that too many people are accepted in higher education outlets today for reasons not related to their GPA but to the school's bottom line of enrollment numbers. A door has been opened for them, but they have to push themselves through it and are responsible for moving ahead. Be proud of your status as a college student, but be aware of how much accountability comes with that label.

You were raised with common sense and good examples so I doubt you'll fall into the trap of over-confidence. Yet, I've seen it happen. You know one of my favorite Bible quotes because you've certainly heard it from me enough times – Whatever you do, work at it with all your heart, as working for the Lord, not for men, (Colossians 3:23) - that is so applicable here. God granted you intelligence, and it is your obligation to apply it. College can and should be fun, but it is hard work. There will be times when you are too tired to study anymore, yet you do; when homework takes precedence over socializing; and when you feel you can't cram another concept into your tired brain, yet you will.

You've heard me cheerlead for college before; indulge me one more time here. I hope you are enthralled with the entire college package – not just the studies but the exposure to people whose backgrounds and lifestyles are outside your familiarity. Open your mind to new perspectives. If I had to define the greatest lesson that college teaches I'd state that it is the ability to think openly. You'll be expected to analyze some of your pre-existing outlooks, question long-standing ideas, view events and situations from different angles. Good! Perhaps many of your opinions will not change, but you'll understand yourself better through them once you've scrutinized why you think or feel that way. Or maybe you'll discover a desire to seek answers in new directions. A solid college education will provide you with the mental tools to search alternatives or strengthen beliefs. Your faith, which already nurtures your spiritual growth, will nourish your mental development as well. I wish you God's sustenance and my personal encouragement in your quest for knowledge.

Sincerely,

A Family Member

Dear Cherished Friends,

"Being confident of this, that He who began a good work in you will carry it on to completion until the day of Christ Jesus." Philippians 1:6

The good work began in me when I was eleven years old. I was not brought up in church, and by the time I was in fifth grade, I still had no idea of the meaning of Christmas or Easter except for Santa Claus and the Easter bunny. When two of my school friends, in an effort to evangelize me, began asking if I knew the meaning of Good Friday, I feigned a stomachache and the teacher had to call for my father to come take me home from school. I was so embarrassed to be so ignorant.

Thanks to our neighbors, a middle-aged couple who invited me to ride with them to Sunday School, I began attending the little country church in our community around that time. It was there that I first heard the message of salvation and invited the Lord into my life during Vacation Bible School. I distinctly remember feeling brand new the next day as I went for a walk to think about what had transpired. I was baptized by immersion when I was thirteen. I began to pray for my mother and father, and I still remember the joy of praying with my mother as she asked Jesus into her life.

I married a local farmer's son, a born-again believer, and we raised our family in the church. We were happily involved in the activities there. One by one, our children became believers as well.

But then, a wrong turn…

After the nest emptied, I found a job and joined a professional organization. I soon found myself becoming restless and enamored of worldly things. My husband and I were growing apart, certainly not his fault. I questioned his judgment, opened my own checking account, and spent money on whatsoever I desired, all under the guise of 'I deserve it.'

Conflicting voices within my head were vying for my attention. I had relegated God to the back burner of my life, having a form of godliness, attending church, singing the hymns, pretending everything was perfect. Yet the shackles were becoming heavier by the day. In private conversations with my husband, I questioned the Scriptures, cast doubt on their infallibility, argued over everything and disagreed with some of the basic tenets of faith to which I had previously held. I was a mess. When I awakened in the night, I could feel an oppressive presence in the room. I believe that Satan was battling for my allegiance. I thought I would find happiness and satisfaction in my new, liberated life, but such was not the case. I became ever more and more despondent, to the point where I would just as soon have ended my life. What a paradox.

Eventually, I left that job to take a position at a retail chain, a move that I soon realized was orchestrated by God and an answer to my husband's prayers. At the time, I thought it merely a coincidence that a friend, with whom I was having lunch, mentioned a position that needed to be filled. She was working for the search firm engaged to fill the position.

"Where is the company located?" I asked.

When she told me, I realized the company was closer to my home, so I expressed interest in interviewing for the job. The interview took place, and I was hired. I suddenly began to hear the voice of

God once again. The owner of the company was truly a servant leader who loved God and exemplified a strong faith.

The time came when I repented with bitter tears for my years of estrangement from God and committed the rest of my life to serving Him. My relationship with my husband was restored, thanks to his forbearing faithfulness. As I began to read the Scriptures again, I turned to the book of Jeremiah and personalized some verses there, inserting my name where the phrase 'house of Israel' is used in the following verses: "Go down to the potter's house and there I will give you my message. So I went down to the potter's house, and I saw him working at the wheel. But the pot he was shaping from the clay was marred in his hands; so the potter formed it into another pot, shaping it as seemed best to him. Then the word of the Lord came to me: 'O house of Israel, can I not do with you as this potter does?' declares the Lord. 'Like clay in the hand of the potter, so are you in my hand, O house of Israel'" (Jeremiah 18:2-6).

Regret is a desolate word, but it can be replaced

by the healing words of forgiveness and reconciliation. Today I know this—I am nothing without God. Only His righteousness covers me. Now I can say, wholeheartedly, that I truly love God, His Son Jesus Christ, and His Holy Spirit with all my heart, with all my soul, and with all my mind. Praise be to God.

Your old friend Clay Pot,
Reshaped by the Master's hand

Therefore, since we have been justified through faith,

we have peace with God

through our Lord Jesus Christ.

Romans 5:1

Therefore, there is now no condemnation for those

who are in Christ Jesus.

Romans 8:1

Dear Accident Victim,

You do not know me. The day we met was probably one of the worst days in your life, but I have to let you know just how much God loves you and all that He did to save your life that day. Perhaps you already know Him. If you do, it could be that He wants to remind you of just how much He loves you. It is kind of like that old hymn, "Tell me the story of Jesus, write on my heart every word. Tell me the story most precious, sweetest that ever was heard." This is your story and I have to tell it.

It was a Wednesday afternoon during rush hour. My friend and I were driving back to Jacksonville when you drove past us like we were standing still. A little further up the road, you caught some gravel in the shoulder, bounced off the concrete wall, and flipped your car. You were ejected and landed in the middle of the freeway while your car landed in the far right-hand lane. That's when God showed up on that freeway for you.

As if guided by the hand of God Himself, all the cars around me just slowly began to veer to the left away from where you had landed. As soon as I pulled off the shoulder, my friend jumped out of the car and ran to your side to see if you were okay. She did not look to see that she was running across two lanes of traffic, but all of the vehicles stopped and let her go. Even though you were lying in the middle lane on the freeway, no cars came near you as they drove by. A few men got out of their vehicles and worked to direct traffic around the scene. Other men were working on collecting your belongings from along the road; one man even found and took care of your cat.

After I stopped the car and looked for a first aid kit, I ran to the scene as well. When I arrived, my friend and another gentleman had rolled you onto your back so you could breathe easier. You had landed on your head and had been struggling. People were donating towels out of their vehicles so she had something to hold onto your head with. Another man found a couple of towels and used them to cover you to ensure your dignity remained intact in spite of the horrible injuries you had. Total strangers found the ability to care about something beyond themselves and did everything they could to help.

While she held pressure on your head, the gentleman, a registered nurse who had stopped as well, and I prayed for you. The gentlemen lifted you to heaven unashamedly with his heart and hands raised. Not too long after, one of the men found your wallet – everything intact – and we finally knew your name. While we were standing there waiting for help to arrive, the gentleman stopped praying, very intently looked at me and asked, "Do you see what God did here? Do you see what He did? He sent her four angels!"

Emergency crews finally arrived, took over your care, and airlifted you from the scene. What happened next still amazes me. The gentleman who had stayed with us at the scene the entire time had, actually, been there from the start. He saw the entire crash from start to finish and was able to give the State Troopers a very accurate account of what happened. When they left with you, we were still standing around trying to figure out what we should do next, like there was still something undone and unfinished. The gentleman looked at me, said he was going to go see what else he could do to help, and he started to walk down the road. I turned my head away for just a moment, but when I tuned back, he was gone. I never saw him again.

One of the strange things about all of these events is that my friend was not supposed to be there that day. She usually is off work at 4:30 and is back in Jacksonville by 5:15 or so. There was an emergent patient at work that day, and she did not leave work until 5:00. More than an hour before your accident, God was planning how He was going to work through your situation and be glorified in the actions of the day. By the time we finally arrived back in Jacksonville, it was almost time to go to church. The timing, once again, was perfect. We were able to mobilize a large portion of the body of Christ to pray for you, to keep you lifted up before the Father.

Thanks to social media, more believers thousands of miles away began to pray as well. Everything that day was timed down to the minute. He truly is an on-time God!

As far as we know, with what little information we are able to obtain, you survived the accident, but as we were told several weeks later, you were still in the hospital. What a plan He must have for your life! I do not know if you will ever get to read this letter or if we will ever be able to meet face-to-face, but the story must be told. I hope you know now and understand just how much He loves you.

In His humble service,

A Fellow Traveler on Life's Highway

For I am convinced that
neither death nor life,
neither angels nor demons,
neither the present nor the future,
nor any powers,
neither height nor depth,
nor anything else in all creation,
will be able to separate us
from the love of God
that is in
Christ Jesus our Lord.
Romans 8:38-39

Beloved Friend,

I love you and am so happy our friendship has deepened into something lasting. We've hurt each other in the past and I am so glad that is behind us. I know that I have thoughtlessly said things that hurt you. You carried that pain for a lot of years and I never knew it. In fact, I thought that I was the injured one because of how you shut me out. It took me a long time to recognize that the fault was mine and that you were protecting yourself from more hurts. I can't undo the pain but I need to make sure you know that I am truly sorry. I cherish our friendship and don't want to jeopardize it again by being blind to your tender heart.

But because I love you, I'm taking the risk of writing this letter. I deeply want you to know God's love because only He can heal your hurts. I know that when I talk about Him, you think I'm saying I'm better than you. I confess that I have judged you in the past, and that was part of how I hurt you. But I was not showing God's love when I did that. I hope that He will love you through me now, but I don't want you to judge Him by my actions. He has a lot more work to do in me.

I remember that you loved Him when we were young. You and your husband were excited about the church you were attending. I also remember when you were disillusioned by the pastor's sin, which made you doubt the truths he had taught you about God. That is understandable, but it began a lifetime of hurt that you still hold within you.

To protect yourself, you shut out most people. I'm grateful to be one of the ones you have let in, and I constantly pray that God will help me to love you tenderly and never again hurt you. I know how fragile your heart is. I've seen some of the bruises and scars you bear.

We have so much in common, so I sometimes wonder what difference it has made in your life to not follow Him. We both have loving husbands, children we care about and the most amazing grandchildren ever. We're content with where our lives have brought us and we each give back to others; I think you do more than I. I'm impressed with how much you do for the elders who have been in your life. You have always been more compassionate.

So how has my walk with Him and yours without Him mattered?

I think the difference is that I have Him to turn to when I need more than the world can offer. I have always had the confidence that my life is good, even when dark times come, because God loves me and He takes care of me. When my son was sick and near death, I turned to Him and was comforted. I knew that He loved us and had plans for our good. He was the one who healed my boy, but I knew that even if the worst happened I would be okay.

You were angry with God when your children went through some difficult times. That was totally understandable. But who did you turn to for comfort? Who did you turn to for healing? Where did you get your hope that it would be okay? I don't think you had hope and I know you haven't healed yet.

My wish for you is that you will find the healing and comfort you've rejected. That instead of turning away from the only One who truly loves you, you will hear His knock, open the door and invite Him in for fellowship over a good meal.

I could tell you about that meal – the bread that is His body, the wine that is His blood – the sacrifice He made for you to be able to fellowship with Him. But I know you know that truth and I don't know how to tell it to you without sounding like I'm preaching at you. I don't want to preach.

I just want you to find the love that only He can give you. I'm sending this letter with trepidation, but also with hope and my deepest love.

I'm waiting for you by His side, so we can share that meal with Him together.

Much love,

Your Caring Friend

Dear One,

I never thought my testimony was all that exciting. I was the goody-goody who accepted Christ as a child, growing up in a Christian home. However, I have been able to see God's hand at work in my life and that is what I want to share with you today, for His hand is at work in your life, too, even if you can't see it just yet.

Who would have thought that my skipping a grade in school had anything to do with my mother's death? Now, years later, I see that the two events were uniquely woven together by the hand of God.

It is true; I did well in school and skipped 8th grade. In my 9th grade year, I started dating the man who would become my husband. Yes, I was young. I was only 14 at the time, but it was all a part of God's greater plan. On my 16th birthday, he gave me a ring. Yes, I was still very young, but when you allow God to work, all the pieces of the puzzle fit perfectly together.

After high school graduation, I went off to college. We both made it through those years unscathed because we allowed God to be the center of our relationship. Many people said we wouldn't last because we were too young and because I would fall in love with someone else during our separation, but they were wrong.

The wedding took place shortly after college. The date my husband first asked me to go out happened to fall on a Saturday that year. This is just one more way I could later see God's hand at work, it wasn't just coincidence.

We planned waiting a year or so before starting a family, but that was not to be. Three weeks after the wedding I was so sick and knew I was pregnant. Nine months and two days after we got married, we brought our first daughter into the world. Our daughter was the first grandchild. I knew people were mentally counting out the months, but no one could see what God had in store just yet. His timing is always perfect.

Nine months after the birth of my daughter, my mother found out she had breast cancer. It had spread throughout her body and the doctors were not optimistic. Four months into her illness, our home church purchased airline tickets so my daughter and I could visit. It was during that visit that the culmination of God at work came to be. My daughter, who was just over a year old, began taking her first steps. My mother, as ill as she was, was overjoyed to see that. Two weeks later, my mother was gone.

I believe that God was blessing her by allowing her to witness the first steps of the only grandchild she would ever have the pleasure of holding. That would not have been possible if God had not already been at work for years. If I had not skipped a grade, I would have graduated a year later, gone to college a year later, got married a year later, and had a child a year later. A year later would have been too late for my mom.

God knows every minute detail of our lives. He knows exactly the moments we are struggling. He knows the heartache we feel. All of those things can truly work together for our good, even if nothing good seems to be happening in your life at the moment. Some day, though, you will be able to see a pattern in your life as well.

Dear One, in the midst of everyday life you may

not be able to see exactly how God is working, but you can be assured of at least one thing: God loves you. He so badly wants to be a part of your life so He can show you where He is working. All you have to do is call out His name in earnest and He will answer. Call to Him today, Dear One.

Love,

Forever in His Hands

Dear Younger Self,

You are now young, happy, and pure, and about to make the biggest mistake of your life. You will carry on making another, and another. My letter cannot prevent your fall. I cannot stop you from finding trouble and pain.

But I can give you hope. I can tell you there is One who loves you, who pursues you, and who has always been with you though you have not recognized Him. This One will never leave you. His pursuit will endure in the years to come when you fall, and while you ignore Him. He is God who made you and who loves you and who will be with you when you come of age and believe you have moved beyond your past, and when you enter marriage with a happy sort of blindness, looking forward to sweet notions of motherhood.

Brace yourself, for the road ahead will be difficult. You will suffer a miscarriage. People will tell you one miscarriage is common. They will tell you not to worry. Then you will suffer a second miscarriage, and a third. Doctors will identify you as a Habitual Aborter, a common label for women who have had three or more miscarriages. You will suffer a fourth and fifth miscarriage and these will be the most miserable years of your life. You will not realize it, but God will be there. You will believe these troubles are punishment for the horrible actions of your past and still, God will be there. You will doubt your credibility as a woman (as a person even!) You will visit too many doctors, have too many examinations, and cry too many tears. You will despise yourself and you will try to self-destruct.

During this time large groups of prayer warriors will form. It will begin with two loved ones who have prayed for you. You will be unaware that these two have told friends who have also told friends, who have enlisted women's prayer group ministries and entire church congregations to pray for you. These people—most of whom do not know you and all of them knowing you are not a believer—will love you tenderly through their prayers, and God will be there.

On the day your son is born, there will be a moment when his perfect little body is resting against your raised legs. You will look at your son and see the way he stares back at you with his wide glistening eyes. In this moment, you will be in awe and you will know there exists something greater than man. You won't be able to explain it. You will simply know. You will not know what that thing is yet and I want to tell you so that it won't take so long for you to figure it out, but who am I kidding? You are a stubborn one and it will take as long as it takes regardless of my letter. Meanwhile, every night before you go to sleep for years to come, you will whisper sincere gratitude to this great thing.

After the birth of your daughter and several more years you will continue to 'give thanks' to this great thing. You will find yourself in the midst of a couple of lovely friends who happen to be Christian. Stay with them. Hang out with them as often as possible. These lovely friends will feed you nourishment and warmth, and the seed that was planted inside of you the day your son was born will sprout. Your lovely friends will give you books, which you will consume.

They will give you your very first Bible. Your curiosity will increase and you will ask your friends questions about their Christian faith. They will tell you that you are loved and there are precious gifts waiting for you.

"But how do I get there?" you will ask.

Your lovely friends will answer simply, "The gifts are right in front of you. All you have to do is grab them."

You will wonder how it could be possible that God wants to give you gifts like His grace and His mercy, for free! You will wonder how it could be possible that you don't have to work for it, that all you have to do is repent and accept His son Jesus Christ as your Lord and Savior. Whenever you try to imagine Christ with you, all you will be able to see is a mirror image of yourself, an offensive reflection of your failings. Hang on dear child. Praise God that His patience will outlast your stubborn nature. Eight and half years after the day your son is born and forty–two years after you were born you will unclench your fist, one rigid finger at a time, and you will let go of resistance. You will take a leap of faith into the loving arms of Jesus Christ.

You will learn the meaning of eternal love and your life will never be the same. You will still find trouble and pain, but you will see that suffering alone is poles apart from suffering with Christ and the Holy Spirit at your side. You will understand where it is you will go from here; that life on earth is not an end but a beginning of something much larger. You will find meaning in life on earth.

So carry on with your life, Younger Self. Go ahead and make your mistakes, but never give up. For there is hope in Christ and though it will take you a lifetime to get there, one day you will know Him. You will see Him in your past, present, and future and you will want to share the news of Him with others the way I long to share the news of Him with you.

With deep love,

Your Older Self

Jesus answered,
"I am the way and the truth and the life.
No one comes to the Father
except through me.
John 14:6

Dear Fearful,

I am writing to tell you I know how you feel. That crippling feeling you get where your heart races, your palms sweat, and you feel nauseous. I've been there. I've been there where you feel too confused to make a decision. There were times I couldn't have told you my name.

I've felt the panic sweep over me when my spouse suggests we "go somewhere."

No! I don't wanna go! I wanna stay home!

For home felt safe. No one could see me at home. They don't stare, point, or whisper, "What is WRONG with her?"

I've made the excuses. "I don't feel well," was my favorite. "I'm busy," was another. I've promised to do more things, knowing I'd back out at the end. I've watched the frustration in my family when we couldn't go, didn't go, when I wouldn't go. I've been the barrier and caused the heartache. I sent my husband and daughter to a theme park alone more than once. I stayed home. I was too afraid.

Yes, I've been there. I've been where you feel

the fear choking you. I cried copious tears asking, pleading, "Why, God why?"

One day, I determined, I would have an answer. "I can't live this way!" I wailed.

And God showed me the truth about fear. The truth is, I don't have to live that way. The truth is, when Jesus died on the cross, God set me free. Fear has been defeated forever. The truth is, the devil gives fear, and he is powerless in Christ. I found the truth.

I also found that the road back is hard. There were times I was successful. I pushed through the fear and I rejoiced. My husband said, "See, you did it!" There were also times I gave in and I failed. Once again, the place of success became defeat. It wasn't easy. I had to do the things I was so afraid of doing. I had to "go anyway."

I learned to turn to my spouse for support. Many times, I'd say, "Just keep driving and don't turn around." You see, had it been left up to me, I would have turned around. I would have gone running back to my place of secrecy and pseudo-safety. I could see nothing but the fear.

There is a saying, "You can't win a victory as

long as the problem is the biggest thing in your life."
At one point, fear was the biggest thing. It was larger
than anything I faced at any minute of the day. But
fear isn't truth.

No, truth is God. God is bigger than fear. He is
higher. He is stronger. He is more. God is more than
enough for anything I face in my life. When I made
God bigger, the fear grew smaller. Then one
afternoon, as I sat in my front yard admiring the
flowers, the breeze blowing against my face, I
realized I was happy and began to weep.

"I'm happy! Thank you, God! I'm so happy!"
How did that happen? How did I get to this place of
peace?

How? Through worship. I worshipped daily,
minute by minute. I fell on my face saying, "God, you
are holy. You are mighty. You are all I need." As I
did, His presence filled me. The more time I spent
with Him, the greater He became and the smaller the
problem. Suddenly, I could hear His still small voice.
I knew where to turn. I had Him to rely on. He is ever
faithful.

And freedom came. Today, when the old fears

try to come back, I remember and I stop and I worship. I sing psalms to Him. I remind myself how little I am and how powerful He really is.

Fearful, you don't have to be afraid anymore. God loves you. He loves you despite anything you've done, anywhere you've been, or anything you've come from. He loves you no matter your choices, no matter your family or friends. When you can't see a way out, He has one. Do what I did; ask Him.

"God, I'll do anything, ANYTHING at all, if you'll save me." I meant those words. I practiced them, and He answered.

God's love changed me forever. I am no longer bitter, hateful, lonely, and sad. I am loved. God loves me. My friends love me. My family loves me, and I am eternally grateful.

Yours truly,

Freedom

For it is by grace you have been saved, through faith—and this not from yourselves, it is the gift of God— not by works, so that no one can boast.

Ephesians 2:8-9

Dear Children,

Your mother is very ill. The doctors tell her that it's terminal. We adults know what that means or what it could mean. Yet, what could that possibly mean to you three? Yes, there are those adults who as young children had a mother with a terminal illness. They remember. They know. Those are the ones that could tell you how sad and scary it feels. Grandpa knows. His mother died when he was 11-years- old. But, yes, you're right. It's your mother, the woman you call mom, and no one else's. We know that, but someone knows it exactly and perfectly. Jesus knows. Jesus knows your mom inside and out. He loves her very much. You want to know what's happening to your mom. You want Jesus to make her better. That's okay. It's okay to have thoughts and feelings like that. I, too, want and feel the same thing.

Children, I'm sorry, I can't make your mom better, but I can love you. Love. Remember that love is the right way. When Jesus walked the earth, He spoke so much about love. He taught us that this is the most important thing in life. Remember how your mom taught you that Jesus died for each one of you because of love? If you lived at that time, and you had been the only person on earth, He would've died just for you.

Children, this is the love, His love, that will help you along your journey together. You know how your mom used to hold you in her arms and rock you? Can you picture Jesus rocking your mom? Well, it's true. Jesus reaches down into your mom's heart and rocks it gently and comforts her. He was the first ever to love her, and He will never leave her. Children, your mom loves you very much. Jesus loves you very much. I love you very much.

Do you remember all the miracles that Jesus performed in the Bible? He changed water into wine, raised His dear friend Lazarus from the dead, and He even walked on water. Yes, it's okay to want a miracle for your mom. It's okay to ask Jesus to cure your mom. In the end, He knows what He has to do. In the end, we have to trust His decision. I don't know what He'll decide, but I do know that He wants to hear your prayers. In Luke's writings, we read about Jesus telling His disciples how much He

wanted the children near. He doted on them. He loved
their purity and willingness to learn and understand.
He waits for you to go to Him with your tears about
your mom. He wants nothing but to comfort you and
strengthen you in your sorrow. His own words tell
you that He'll never leave you or your dad. He'll
never leave your mom. She'll be okay. No matter
what happens, she'll be okay. How do I know this?
Because Jesus is our Savior and gentle brother. Now,
children, go to Him in your mind's eye. Go and rest
your head against His heart. Can you feel His warm
arms wrapped around you and cradling you? He
wipes away all of your tears. How do I know? It's
because He told us so in the Gospels. Go children,
gather up the Bible and read through its pages. See
the Jesus who longs to comfort. Ask Him to help you.
Don't be afraid children. It'll work. I promise.

With all my Love,

Your forever Aunt

"For God so loved the world that he gave his one and only Son, that whoever believes in him shall not perish but have eternal life. For God did not send his Son into the world to condemn the world, but to save the world through him. Whoever believes in him is not condemned, but whoever does not believe stands condemned already because he has not believed in the name of God's one and only Son."

John 3:16-18

Therefore, if anyone is in Christ,
he is a new creation;
the old has gone,
the new has come!

2 Corinthians 5:17

Dear Son,

Life hits us hard sometimes, doesn't it? Although I know you are angry right now, please hear me out.

We all make mistakes. We're human. We screw up. We've all been treated badly by others – stomped on, spit upon, rejected, abandoned in some form or fashion.

But how other people treat us does not make us who we are. It's how we respond to their treatment, how we treat ourselves, and how we let God direct our lives that matters.

You can start over. Millions of people start over every day. You just have to want to.

Jesus came so that we might have life – life more abundantly. He died for you, just as He died for all of us. Confess your sins to Him – He forgives you. He loves you more than you could ever dream or imagine. I understand that you may be ashamed of things you've done, or ashamed about things that have been done to you or against you. I'm so sorry all of this has happened.

But please don't be ashamed of who you are.

God made you – special, unique, precious. Jesus'
blood washes away our filth and makes us new –
makes us whole – makes us beautiful.

Son, it's time to refocus yourself. Reach down
deep inside and stir up the courage that lives within
you. You are worthy of a good life. You are worthy
of happiness. You are worthy of peace and
tranquility. It's time to pull up your bootstraps and
make a beautiful life for yourself. Only you and God
together can do that.

I love you. All of us love you. Please know that –
please believe that.

We'll get through this. We never stop praying for
you.

Love,
Mom

About the Contributors

(in Alphabetical Order)

Nicole Anderson is a medical secretary/transcriptionist who is striving to bring glory and honor to Jesus Christ while learning to revive the passion of writing and transform it into coherent thoughts. She currently resides in Arkansas with her three nieces, one nephew, and two adorable dogs.

Elsi Dodge (Boulder, CO) is a single, retired teacher of children with special needs. She travels in a 30-foot RV, with the dubious assistance of her beagle and a small saber-toothed tiger, cleverly disguised as a tabby cat. She tutors, co-leads Bible study, and works with a church youth group.

www.RVTourist.com/blog

Genia Gilbert retired in small town in southwest Arkansas. She's had articles published in Mature Living magazine, a story in *Life Lessons from Grandparents* book published by Write Integrity Press, and a story in a Faithwriters' book. Her passion is sharing God's touch in everyday life.

Judy Hampton was a popular speaker known for her entertaining speaking style and communication skills. She was a respected international keynote speaker for women's conferences and retreats, and the author of three full-length books.

Annie Keys, award-winning author of eight books, including devotionals and the entertaining series *The Grandma Chronicles*, has served in her church for more than 20 years. A strong Christian, a wife, mother, grandmother, great grandmother, she loves to write and bake. Her favorite color is plaid, and she loves to laugh! She and her husband, Dan, live in Florida. Read her daily devotions at **www.rubberontheroad.org**.

Alyssa Liljequist is a videographer, photographer, and writer who enjoys dancing in her free time. You can find her on Instagram **@alyssaliljequist** and Twitter **@ALiljequist**.

Margaret Marty is a retired wife, mother, grandmother, and professional secretary. She has pursued a memoir writing career in retirement, taking classes and establishing a business, Portraits in Prose. You may e-mail her at **mmarty@northlc.com**.

T. Marie Nantais obtained an English Language and Literature degree, and is a published writer and poet. Several of her stories, articles, and poetry have been published in various family Christian print publications along with general secular print publications and web sites.

Ruth O'Neil, born and raised in upstate New York, attended Houghton College. She has been a freelance writer for more than 20 years, publishing hundreds of articles in dozens of publications. You can visit her at **http://ruths-real-life.blogspot.com** or on her website at **http://ruthoneil.weebly.com**. Ruth spends her spare time quilting, scrapbooking, and camping with her family.

Phee Paradise was blessed to be a missionary kid and loves to share that experience in her writing. In *Miracles at Midnight*, she edited her father's stories about his years on the mission field where he saw God change lives for the Kingdom. Phee has also contributed to several books, including *A Ruby Christmas, A Dozen Apologies, Unlikely Merger* and *Trials and Triumphs*. Look for her new book, *A Sincere Heart*, releasing early 2018. She prays that her work will be used by God to His glory.

Linda Panczner enjoys the challenge of writing for various genres. Each writing venture is a positive experience, whether it is therapeutic, a passage to a new insight, or a chance to share a meaningful anecdote.

Theresa Santy lives with her family on the sunny coast of Southern California, where she can be found wearing jeans and flip-flops year-round. Her first published novel, **On the Edge**, won the 2013 FaithWriters Page Turner Contest, and is available on Amazon. Visit Theresa at **theresasanty.com**.

Nanette Thorsen-Snipes has been writing more than thirty years. Her credits include stories in a number of compilation books, including *Guideposts* and *Chicken Soup for the Soul,* among others. She has published hundreds of articles, devotions, and stories in more than fifty print publications. As a mother of four and grandmother of eight, she tries to give God the glory in all things. Contact her at: **nsnipes@bellsouth.net** or **www.faithworkseditorial.com**.

Suzanne D. Williams, a best-selling author, is a native Floridian, wife, mother, and photographer. She is the author of both nonfiction and fiction books. She writes devotionals and instructional articles for various blogs. She also does graphic design for self-publishing authors. She is co-founder of The Edge. To learn more about what she's doing and check out her extensive catalog of stories, visit **www.feelgoodromance.com**.

Books Published by TMP Books

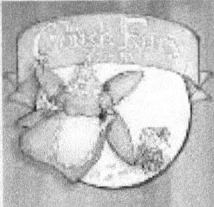
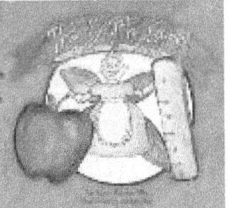

Look for other books

published by

www.TMPbooks.com

Interested in publishing a book?
Visit our website for details.